Peacemaking Without Division:

moving beyond congregational apathy and anger

by Patricia Washburn and Robert Gribbon

The Publications Program of The Alban Institute is assisted by a grant from Trinity Church, New York City.

Copyright 1986 by The Alban Institute, Inc. All rights reserved.

This material may not be photocopied or reproduced in any way without written permission.

Library of Congress Catalog Card # 86-082050

CONTENTS

INTRODUCTION   1

PART I — THE BACKGROUND

A Developmental Approach to Social Issues   3
Three Circles of Action   9

PART II — THE WORKSHOP

Introduction   13
Hopes & Fears   15
Nuclear Stories   17
Bible Reflection   20
Resources for Community Study & Action   22
Conflict and Reconciliation   31
Planning for Peace in the Parish   39
Peacemaking in Worship   42

PART III — THE LEARNINGS

Participant Evaluations   44
The Feminine in Peacemaking   48
Reflections   52

REFERENCES AND FURTHER RESOURCES   55

Foreword

Some church leaders avoid peacemaking programs for fear they will result in congregational warfare. Others anticipate an apathetic response that would only increase their already profound sense of hopelessness. Still others hesitate because they are turned off by guilt-inducing, issue-rattling approaches to social issues—and don't know any alternatives.

If you seek options to "psychic numbing" or fighting over peace, you will want to read this new guide by Patricia Washburn and Robert Gribbon. Here is an approach that moves the issue of peacemaking to the religious level at which churches appropriately work. Moving "beyond information to formation and transformation," the authors' educational approach creates a peacemaking context into which people can bring not only ideas and facts, but their hopes, fears, stories, and commitments. Here is not only a coherent strategy (one that can be adapted to other social issues), but *specific resources*. As you move step-by-step through a Gribbon-Washburn peacemaking workshop, you will learn about conflict management styles that are most effective in peacemaking; how worship should and should not be used; recommended resources for personal, family and community use; effective experiential exercises; and how men and women differ in their approaches to peace. A breakthrough book on effective strategies for non-violent social involvement in the parish, here is an important addition to every minister's bookshelf and every parish library.

Celia Allison Hahn
Director of Publications
The Alban Institute, Inc.

Introduction

This work arises from three convictions. First, congregations ought to be places where people can bring the deepest hopes, fears, and issues of their lives and the times they live in. Second, congregations have an appropriate "religious" way of dealing with issues which is more than simply education or politics. Third, congregations need to be inclusive of great differences of political opinion. This book is about one method of dealing with controversial issues in congregations in non-divisive ways.

We have been concerned because many congregations avoid any controversial issues while others have dealt with issues in limited or divisive ways. For several years we have conducted a number of day-longworkshops on the theme of "Peacemaking without Division" and collected information from the participants. The workshops, based on an explicit model of human development, have been well received and promise one way of approaching issues in non-divisive ways. Although the content issue dealt with here is "peacemaking," with a particular focus on the threat of thermonuclear war, the methodology might be appropriate to other social issues.

This book consists of three parts:

Part I is an overview of the project and an explanation of the developmental theory upon which the approach is based.

Part II is a presentation of the workshop content, a "translation" of the workshop itself from its original interactive oral format to a form accessible to the individual reader.

Part III is a summary of learnings from the project and a reflection on the implications for further work in this area.

This work is not intended to replace the wealth of materials on peacemaking available from secular sources and denominational offices. Our evaluation of the resources, however, suggests that, while they deal with much of the cognitive data of peacemaking, they do not deal with the affective levels of awareness nor the climate within which effective education takes place. The purpose of this work is to help create the congregational *context* in which peacemaking materials and programs may be used.

We hereby express our profound gratitude to all those who have labored in this field and upon whose work we have drawn. Many people have contributed to our insights, in particular those who formed an informal study group in Washington in the Fall of 1983. Our thanks go also to all those who have participated in these workshops, who have shared their hopes, fears, stories and ideas, who have challenged and supported us. Without them, this work would not have been possible.

Our concern for the issues of war and peace has been inspired in part by the question, "What about the children?" We would therefore like to name the specific children, our own, who have inspired this work: Christopher, Peter, Polly and Cory; Benjamin and Melissa.

This work arises out of personal conviction and history which is frequently reflected in the use of the first person. The initials "PW" or "RTG" appear at chapter headings to help the reader identify the particular author speaking. The authors, Patricia Washburn and Robert T. Gribbon, have conducted this series of workshops on "Peacemaking Without Division" for several hundred people and have collaborated in producing a study guide on the nuclear dilemma for the Episcopal Diocese of Washington. Pat Washburn is Assistant Professor for Peace with Justice Studies at the Earlham School of Religion and was previously director of public education for the U.S. Peace Academy Campaign and a "Fellow" at the Churches Center for Theology and Public Policy. Bob Gribbon is an ordained Episcopal priest and Director of Education and Research for The Alban Institute. He directed the Young Adult Ministry Project of The Alban Institute and worked extensively with both campus and military chaplains.

The Alban Institute, Inc. is a non-profit, independent agency dedicated to the health of local religious congregations in all denominations. For information on the availability of the workshops and publications call (202) 244-7320 or write: The Alban Institute, 4125 Nebraska Ave, NW, Washington, DC 20016.

PART I—The Background

A Developmental Approach to the Issues of Peace
(RTG)

The thought of the church dealing with "social issues" sets off tremors in some congregations. Often issues are avoided to prevent conflict and polarization in the church. However, it is our conviction that the local church ought to be, and can be, a place where people can bring the deepest issues of their lives. Too often, the fear of controversy prevents this, undermines both pastoral and prophetic ministry, and robs the congregation of vital energies. How can controversial public issues be engaged in ways that enhance congregational life? What tools or approaches might help congregations deal with issues, specifically with "peacemaking" issues?

Peacemaking, especially the nuclear issue, is a prime example of a public issue with religious dimensions. The threat of nuclear war instills debilitating fear in many; the billions of dollars spent on preparation for nuclear war and the policy of keeping peace by threatening to destroy millions of people present complex moral dilemmas. There are other social issues, but this one touches all people, and may relativize other issues. For example, one of America's outstanding historians was asked what he saw as the greatest threat to the movement for gay rights in the last decades of the twentieth century. He answered simply, "Thermonuclear war." We are all equals under the threat. Peace issues have rapidly gained prominence recently in mainline churches. The past few years have seen the Roman Catholic Bishops' Pastoral letter, the Presbyterian emphasis on peacemaking as the believer's calling, a major document from the United Methodist Church, and countless other actions at church judicatory levels. We see little of this being translated into sustained visible activity in local congregations.

How can the congregation be a place where people can express the concerns of living in a nuclear age? Since 1983, we have been experimenting and collecting data through a workshop called "Peacemaking without Division." The basic purpose is to share approaches for dealing with "peacemaking" themes in congregational life rather than to present data about the issues. Offered primarily on Saturday and Sunday afternoons to allow both clergy and lay participation, the workshops have been used in both denominational and ecumenical settings. The format includes brief presentations and experiential exercises based on an explicit model of human development, a theoretical tool for understanding our attempts to work with controversial themes in congregational life.

Usually, we present the theory to workshop participants after moving through the following five major steps:
Exploring hopes and fears;
Telling personal stories;
Doing Bible study;
Using denominational resources;
Applying Conflict Management tools.
We find explaining the theory after the experience to be the most effective educational approach. However, in some settings with low trust levels or very limited time for a presentation, we have shared the theory first and then asked people to participate in at least some brief structured experience.

The developmental theory is presented here with examples related to the peace issue, but the general theory is applicable to many issues. As presented, the theory is a skeleton, an extreme simplification in which the reader may recognize human development theory from Piaget, Erikson, Kohlberg, Gilligan, Fowler, Kegan and others. To simplify that research, we might think of four levels of awareness that build on one another: FEELINGS, STORY, COMMUNITY, IDEAS.

Feelings

From our birth, we all respond to the world with feelings—pain/pleasure, security/insecurity, hope/fear, etc. At times the feelings form images in or projected beyond the mind. One favorite story is of young Tommy who hads been put to bed several times. When he cried out again, his father with some anger went into Tommy's room and asked what the matter was. "I'm scared," said Tommy, "there are bears in here." "Well," said the father, turning on the light, "you can see that there aren't any bears." Replied Tommy, "Of course not when you turn the light on."

As we grow, we build on the feelings, but the feelings are basic and probably shape the tone and content of what we later express in thoughts.

In the workshop, we first identify what our hopes and fears are for the congregation. This is, in part, a planning piece. Once we have named what we hope for, or what we are afraid might happen, we can later plan what to do. But, particularly as we move to the personal level, we must acknowledge that hopes and fears are *real*, even when they may not be realistic. If someone says that they are afraid of the Russians, or afraid of a nuclear accident, we need to hear and acknowledge that fear.

Story

As we begin to make sense of the world as well as react to it, we do this first in the form of narrative, of story. We make connections between what we do and what others do. In childhood and in primitive religion the activity of the world is attributed to our own actions and the actions of other, more powerful beings in a rough ordering of cause and effect. We are nurtured by the stories told to us and we tell stories. The full flower of the narrative stage usually comes around age twelve. If as a parent or teacher you ask a ten-year-old "What happened?" you will get a story. If you interrupt and say "Get to the point—what happened?" he or she will often start the story again from the beginning: that is the way a 10 year old makes sense of the world. But all of us retain the story-telling mode. Some of us will stay up late at night turning pages to find out "what happens next." Good speakers and preachers will tell you the power of stories for every age group - when you tell stories, you can see people visibly relax and adopt a different posture.

In the workshop, participants share part of their own story of what it has been like to live in a nuclear age. In the process of telling our nuclear stories, we both acknowledge some of our personal hopes and fears and begin to understand the experience of those who disagree with us. We acknowledge that the story of the nuclear age is a story which we all share. It begins to make "the problem" a shared experience. (For a further description of "nuclear stories" see *Action Information*, Mar/Apr 1983, "A safe place to face our nuclear terror." See appendix.)

We continue to build on the story-telling stage in the Bible study. In Christian settings, we usually use the post-resurrection story in which Jesus appears granting peace to the disciples when they are gathered in fear behind locked doors (John 20:19-23). We use this passage as a story which speaks to our experience of fear and hope. This is very different from using the Bible as a proof-text or basis for discussion. We use it as a shared story which is also a part of our communal experience.

Community

Beyond the level of the individual story (and all these stages overlap) we understand ourselves as human beings by belonging, by being members of a community. Community incorporates both the power of face-to-face relationships and the power of rules and norms. We tend to trust information from people we know. Right and wrong tend to be identified with community norms, "the way we do things." Authority is granted to recognized leaders of the community. There is often discomfort with challenges to, or changes in, that authority. Our values and beliefs tend to be formed by the groups we belong to. Identity, even one's identity in faith, tends to be bound up with the groups in which we participate; thus to the question "Are you a Christian?" the response may be, "Yes, I'm a member of First Church on the corner."

The personal storytelling in small groups is a communal experience as is the Bible study. We continue to build on the communal stage by looking at authoritative statements and resources on social issues from the churches. There may be disagreement about the content of particular statements, but in each case we can say, "These are statements from authorities in our community, and we ought to at least make an effort to find out what they are saying." Other communal resources include work in small groups, activities for families, and agencies for action within the system.

Ideas and opinions

Experiences away from home or outside of our communities and the development of our critical thinking ability may lead us to distinguish our own opinions from those of the community. This level of ideas tends to be more individualistic and rationalistic. We are able to debate our own opinions on rational grounds and may be quite critical of the commonly held opinions of our community. Many a college freshman new to this level of awareness has explained the "right" way of viewing the world to bemused parents.

To deal with the level of ideas and disagreement in the church, and to help people who operate primarily in this stage to engage other persons within a church setting, we introduce some of the concepts of conflict management, especially tools to help people move from a paradigm of win/lose to win/win. We know that many churches avoid any topic on which people might disagree because they have a "no-conflict norm," that is, an unwritten rule that "we never disagree here." We point to some tools for dealing with conflict in other ways than avoidance. Of course, the whole workshop is designed to help people identify common feelings, stories, and community loyalties before dealing at the level of ideas and strategies.

After a brief discussion of peacemaking activities in worship, the workshop participants join in worship which pulls together all the activity of the day. Worship also points to a level of awareness beyond the four we have mentioned. In time, we learn that all symbols are multi-dimensional, and life presents mystery beyond our ability to explain or articulate.

Congregations are particularly equipped to help people relate their lives to the unseen mystery; they need not become simply educational or political institutions. However, when churches deal with social issues, they often begin at the level of ideas and opinions. The issue is introduced into an adult study group or forum, often in the form of a debate which guarantees that it will be dealt with at the level of opinions and that there will be disagreement. On the other hand, activist groups sometimes bombard people at the feeling level, trying to move people to action through fear or guilt. However, we add to the brokenness of the world when we act from fear. We create new enemies, we become driven by that "fear which has torment, rather than the love which makes us fearless." One great contribution of the church to the world order can be to help people move from fear to hope as a basis for action.

There has been positive response to the workshops from a variety of people—longtime activists, cautious clergy, conservative laymen. The workshops offer little comfort to those who insist that the church should take a particular political stance. But pastoral and prophetic ministry need not be at odds. Issues affect people, and people bring the issues. If we take individuals seriously, we will create contexts into which people can bring all their hopes, fears, stories, commitments, and ideas. When we allow all of reality to be dealt with in the religious context we find that both issues and people are transformed.

As a way to begin that process of contextualizing, it is perhaps helpful to begin with a biblical image that we use throughout our work.It is important to remember that when lay people approach an issue or come to a workshop within a church context, they always come from some Biblical vision or faith conviction, however inarticulate that may be. They come as volunteers, not because they have to, and bring personal concerns and hopes for growth as well as concerns for their congregation. With this in mind, we begin each workshop with a period of recollection and silent prayer, and a brief reflection on the connections between the personal and the global issues entitled the "Three Circles of Action."

Three Circles of Action
(PW)

The prophet Micah teaches us both the promise and the responsibility of our task of reconciliation. In Chapter 4 we are told that God will "mediate" disputes between peoples, will "disarm" the nations, and will bring justice and "allocation of scarce resources".

> "God will judge between great peoples
> and make decision between nations far and wide.
> and they shall hammer their swords into plowshares,
> And their spears into pruning hooks.
> Nation shall lift no sword against nation,
> And never again will they learn to make war.
> Every one shall live beneath the shade of their own vine and fig tree, and none shall make them afraid."

Chapter 6, verse 8, in turn reminds us of the responsibility we have to bring this "peaceable kingdom" into being.

> "For What does the Lord require of you;
> To Act justly, to love constantly, and to walk humbly with your God."

Micah's three requirements are one way to envision our task. Let us first illustrate the three levels of peacemaking/reconciliation.

We are called to peacemaking on three levels, and the imagery of the radiating circles is a helpful one for me. The first level, the Personal, coincides with learning to walk humbly with God; the second or Inter-Personal level is the one at which we do most of our work, where we learn to love constantly; and finally in the outermost circle, at the Transpersonal level, we are called to move beyond our closer community to the larger world community where

we act on behalf of the justice claims of all our brothers and sisters.

Here are some examples of how that task is lived out on each of the levels and how each level of peacemaking is connected and interwoven with the others.

Personal Peacemaking—Living from the Center

Much of the contemplative literature from both our own and the Eastern meditative traditions calls us back to the inner life, the center from which all action flows. In the Quaker tradition it is the realm of the "inner light." Psychological language speaks of wholeness, centering and individuation. That sense of inner connectedness is essential to all peacemaking. Thomas Kelly says in his *Testament of Devotion*, "The experience of the Presence is the experience of peace, and the experience of peace is the experience not of inaction but of power, and the experience of power is the experience of a pursuing Love that loves its way untiringly to victory. One who knows the Presence knows peace, and s/he who knows peace knows power and walks in complete faith that that objective Power and Love which has overtaken us will overcome the world." (Kelly, 1941, p.174) Art Simon, author of "Bread for the World," and brother of Senator Paul Simon, states: "Christians are twice-converted people. They are first converted from the world to Jesus Christ, but then they are converted back to the world again, to love the world and relate to the world, no longer as before but now through the heart and mind of Christ." (Simon, 1985) Thus, living out of the Center ultimately brings us back into community.

The Interpersonal—Living in Community

Most of our peacemaking is done in community with others, our "families, friends and neighbors, and those who are alone." For many of us the church or our own community organizations are the focus of much of our work. It is here that we learn to love constantly, to love our neighbors, and perhaps to love those with whom we have conflicts (our enemies). Let me share an example out of my own recent experience. I am now on the faculty of the Earlham School of Religion teaching and coordinating their peace and social justice ministry program. In a sense I am attempting to equip my students to work in that third circle of doing Justice. But before I could accept the "call" to Earlham I had to do some major reconciliation in my own family with my two teenage daughters. Any of us who have been parents know that the family is a "culture medium" for peacemaking, for the ministry of reconciliation. Often we neglect to give ourselves credit for the works of peace that we do each day in loving, nurturing and supporting our family and friends. Many persons who do not consider themselves activists are willing to make a statement about what they celebrate and find as a "hopeful sign" in their own lives and their own communities. Learning to love one's neighbor and the gifts and graces which that neighbor brings to our lives is a major task of peacemaking. Realistically we are not always in "love and charity with our neighbor" and thus it is important to know some of the tools and techniques of conflict management.

Our final requirement is to ACT JUSTLY. When we ask the question "Who is a member of my family? How large is my community?" that question then links our concern for the interpersonal with the transpersonal.

The Transpersonal—Living as Co-Creators

The Transpersonal realm moves us beyond the local to the global and systemic concerns where often we find peacemaking linked with justice. "There can be no peace without justice" is a theme running through much of the work of many of our denominations. As we extend our understanding of family, we begin to see the linkages between our local communities and the world. We have seen injustice in the deterioration of our core cities and the higher unemployment rates among uneducated and minority peoples. One of the ways our awareness has been sharpened in our churches recently is the experience of a number of our "family" members who have become concerned and have made trips with other church folk to Latin America or the USSR and who upon returning have told their stories. Desmond Tutu and other church leaders from South Africa have made us more aware of the evil of apartheid. In all these situations the frustrations associated with injustices bring fear and an escalating "spiral of conflict," as my friend Mike Mapes of the US Peace Academy Campaign used to say. Our task is to break that spiral before it escalates to violence. One of the ways we do that both at the local and the global levels is by learning our own conflict styles and some of the tools of conflict management (which we will address later).

When I first began working in Washington as a lobbyist, I remember my mother being aghast and wondering how she had failed in her parenting. For me, it was a logical step in a life journey that had moved me from my own "personal" struggle for inner peace out into the "interpersonal" realm as a wife, mother, and grandmother, and ultimately to "transpersonal" or global concerns. One of the major life events for me was becoming a grandmother. I realized at that moment that I wanted my grandson, Paul, to have the same quality of life and opportunity for the future that I had been given as a child. It was a moment of connecting my past, my present, and my hope for the future. In the workshops, I often ask, "What about the children?" and carry a small totem, a baby sock (left by Paul on a recent visit) to remind myself that the work for peace is a part of a dynamic that encompasses life from the most personal to the most global.

PART II—The Workshop

Introduction

Having created the context for the work, and carrying with us both our imagery of the three circles of action (personal/interpersonal/transpersonal) and the four levels of learning (feelings/story/community/ideas) let us now move into a simulated workshop mode and begin to work on methods of peacemaking without division in the local church. The workshop begins with a brief period of Quaker silence followed by the description of the three circles of action, and a presentation of the agenda for the day. As a reader, you have the advantage of having read about the four levels of learning. In the workshop, the day's agenda progresses through the levels of learning, but the theory is presented to participants at the end of the day.

The "Peacemaking Without Division" workshops have been personal, interactive, communal experiences. In order to preserve as much of that flavor as possible in a book, as well as to show you what happens, we have chosen to address you in this section as we might address participants in a workshop beginning at 9:00 on a Saturday morning in a church hall. We invite you to participate, and then later to adapt any of this to your own needs.

AGENDA
Hopes and Fears (30 minutes)
Nuclear Stories (45 minutes)
   BREAK
Bible Study (30 minutes)
Using denominational statements & resources (45 minutes)
   BREAK for lunch and browsing resources
Conflict Management Tools (45 minutes)
Planning for Peace in the Parish (45 minutes)
Worship and Dismissal (15 to 30 minutes)

Here is our agenda for the day, I want to give you a quick overview before we begin. We've put approximate times on this, but we can be a bit flexible. We are trying to crowd a lot into a brief period of time, and our purpose is to give you a taste of some things that you can use in your congregation. You could use more time on any of these sections, and throughout the day you will find that just as you've gotten interested in an exercise, we're interrupting you to move on to the next.

Throughout the workshop, we will be learning from our own experience, sharing with others and looking at global issues. We expect that you will gain personal insights, tools for use in your congregation, and some new approaches to international concerns.

Hopes and Fears (Unit 1)
(RTG)

I'm a researcher with The Alban Institute, which is concerned with the effective functioning of congregations and their quality of life. Part of my concern in the area of "peacemaking" in congregations grew out of a project I did several years ago in which we interviewed over a hundred people in churches all around the country. We were concerned to see if and how members of the "baby-boom" generation might be coming back to church. One theory was that those people who had been involved in social protest during the 1960's might come back to churches that were involved with social issues. We found very few congregations or individuals involved with social issues—those who had chosen to engage in local programs of direct service.

We also noticed something else. Near the end of an extended personal interview in a comfortable church setting, we asked people a very direct question, "When you think about the future—for yourself, for the people you care about, for the world—is there anything that makes you anxious or uneasy?" Out of 103 individual interviews, only 3 mentioned war or the nuclear threat. Were people unable to think about these things or unable to talk about them in church?

In recent years many denominations have produced statements, programs, and resources on peacemaking, but we see little use of these in local congregations. Why is it that congregations aren't involved in social issues, don't enable people to express concern about a global threat, and don't use the materials on peace produced by their denomination? As we asked these questions, we found that some "social activists" had very unrealistic expectations about congregations, and many congregational leaders were fearful of what would happen if they were to deal with "controversial issues" in the congregation.

You are probably involved in this workshop because you would like to see something happen in your congregation around the issue of peace or peacemaking. At this point, we'd like to ask you to take a card and write down what you'd like to see happen in your congregation—what are your hopes? (3 minutes) Now, turn the card over and write on the other side what you are afraid may happen. What are your fears for your congregation? (3 minutes)

At this point, workshop participants introduce themselves briefly, giving name, where they are from, and whatever they would like to tell about their hopes and fears for their congregation. For some of the hopes and fears of others, see box below.

Hopes & Fears - Research Feedback

What would you like to have happen in your congregation around the issue of peace? What are you afraid may happen? We have asked those questions of several hundred clergy and laypeople attending workshops on "peacemaking without division." While we asked about both hopes and fears, the fears stand out most clearly—most frequently the fear of polarization and anger or, for activists, the fear that apathy will dominate, "nothing will happen." See below for other responses.

What I am Afraid May Happen...

Selected responses from laity:

- I'm afraid that there would be such discord raised that the congregation would come apart and the people who vehemently disagree would leave.
- Afraid that I will burn out and drop out.
- People will become defensive, think we are not patriotic or think we are "soft-headed, naive idealists."
- We will deal in generalities, reach no conclusions, retreat into idealistic views.
- I am afraid that the rector will not provide adequate leadership, even though he may personally favor the effort.

Selected responses of clergy:

- I'm afraid of personal rejection, people leaving the parish.
- Congregation will split along ideological lines.
- My leading where no one will follow.
- Fear "creating waves" will abort significant and substantial contributions to larger church and community.

Nuclear Stories (Unit 2)
(PW)

Earlier Bob Gribbon mentioned that one of the motivations for his involvement with this work was his surprise that so few people mentioned their "fears" of nuclear war even when directly asked. This phenomenon appears to be an example of what Robert Jay Lifton has described as "psychic numbing." He explains that when the possibility of extinction is too overwhelming to us, we block it out and go on about business as usual. One of the most important pastoral tasks we can undertake is to help people tell their stories and break the silence.

Joanna Rogers Macy has written a book entitled *Despair and Personal Power in the Nuclear Age* in which she suggests that we must go through a process of grieving akin to what Dr. Elisabeth Kubler Ross has described in her work on death and dying. Macy says that this work "refers to the psychological and spiritual work of dealing with our knowledge and feelings about the present planetary crisis in ways that release energy and vision for creative response." There is a need to do our own grief work, to move from despair to "empowerment," which as a Christian I would call hope. That process is the essential first step toward becoming able to deal with our hopes and fears in ways that free us to go forth in peace to love and to serve the God of Creation.

One of the exercises in Joanna Macy's book is called "telling our nuclear stories." We have all grown up under the nuclear shadow, but we don't talk about our common story. This story is shared by all of us and it is important both to tell our own story and to hear the stories of others. Let me begin by sharing a bit of my own story and then invite each of you to spend about 15 minutes in groups of three, telling and listening to each other.

Pat's nuclear story:

I am complicit. My family helped to build the bomb. That is a major piece of my nuclear story. The evening before I was to leave for college, my father called me into his study, and I thought to myself, "Here comes the sex lecture." But he was not concerned about my libido; he was concerned that I not join any "radical" groups that might jeopardize my uncle's security clearance. My mother's brother was a brilliant young nuclear physicist who worked with Teller and Lawrence to design the nuclear tests in the Pacific in the 1950's. We all considered my uncle to be the family hero. It was only recently that his work came back to haunt me, when we were visited in Washington by a group working with the Marshall Islanders who had suffered long-term radiation effects from those tests and who were lobbying for a Nuclear-Free Pacific.

The next piece of my story is a very personal one. When I was pregnant with my first child, we became aware of the dangers of Strontium 90 in breast milk, and I was torn between nursing and not. I felt impotent and powerless against this air-borne "enemy." It was a painful choice, but I am happy to report that my son is now grown and the father of my wonderful grandson.

Finally, the imminence of the nuclear threat was brought home to me by yet another one of my children, my delightful teenage daughter. Before "The Day After" was on television, we had a family discussion in which I casually asked her, "Do you ever think about the bomb?" She became very grave, unlike her usual bubbly self, and said, "Yes, Mom. I think about the bomb every day." Our children do indeed live under "the nuclear shadow."

Bob's nuclear story:

When I think about this exercise, I think of the everyday things related to life in a nuclear age that we never talk about. What do you think of when you hear a CONELRAD test on the radio or hear an air-raid siren? When I was a kid in school we used to do the old "duck and cover" drills and practice lining up against the lockers in the hall. At that time in the early '50s my family was living in the midwest and we knew a family who had moved to our area from the east coast because of fear of "the A-bomb." Ironically, that area of the country is now part of the ICBM missile fields.

The biggest "nuclear scare" I remember came for many of us who were living on the East coast during the 1962 Cuban missile crisis. I recall college friends who could not study that night because they thought the end was only minutes away.

Part of my story does not directly involve nuclear weapons. I've worked with those in West Germany whose daily duty is along the armed wall that denies political freedom to the people of the Eastern Block; and I have seen the fences on the Southern border of this country that keep out the poor of the third world. These impressions too are part of our experience of living in a nuclear age and "cold" war.

I find that as we listen to the stories of those who differ from us, we come to a better understanding and appreciation of them and the experiences that inform their views. This exercise of "nuclear story-telling" is not a time to argue about those views or the political conclusions people may have drawn from their experiences. Rather this is a time to sit close, listen attentively, and hear the stories of what it has been like for others to live in a time of "non-peace" under the nuclear shadow.

All of the groups meet in the same room, pulling their chairs around. At the close of the nuclear story telling, we do a bit of "debriefing," sharing a few insights gained or questions raised with the whole group and we pass out the article on nuclear story-telling which is found in the appendix of this book. After a break, we ask each group of three to join with another group for the Biblical Reflection.

The preceding exercise uses the story-telling form as a way in which some personal fears can be shared and an awareness of shared history can be built. The next exercise, a guided meditation on a Bible story, uses the story-telling mode as a vehicle to help us move from fear to hope.

Biblical Reflection (Unit 3)
(RTG)

Form groups of six people in circles and listen to this passage from John's gospel several times. Take a deep breath, relax, and let your mind travel to another time and place.

> "Then the same day at evening, being the first day of the week, when the doors were shut where the disciples were assembled for fear of the authorities, Jesus came and stood in their midst and said, 'Peace be unto you.'
> And when he had so said, he showed them his hands and his side. Then were the disciples glad when they saw the Lord.
> Then said Jesus to them again, 'Peace be unto you: as my father has sent me, even so send I you.'
> And when he had said this, he breathed on them, and said, 'Receive the Holy Spirit: whosoever sins you forgive, they are forgiven, and whosoever sins you retain, they are retained."'
> (John 20:19-23)

Imagine yourself as one of the disciples in first century Palestine. Imagine a room with a single door, tightly barred. The one whom you have followed for nearly three years, the one you have set your hopes on, has been suddenly taken from you, and crucified. It is all over. Experience the feelings of shock, grief, confusion, disorientation, fear. "They" may be coming after you.

Consider the locked door. What might lie beyond it out in the city? Can you name any of the fears against which that door is barred?

Suddenly, Jesus is with you. "Peace be with you," he says, and shows the marks, the proof of who he is. "Then were the disciples glad . . ." Feel the joy, the relief, the release.

He says again, "Peace be with you. As my father has sent me, so I send you. Receive the Holy Spirit." Feel the power of the Spirit, strengthening, sweeping away the fear, sending you out beyond the locked doors, into the city, into all the world.

Still sitting quietly, let your mind now come into the present. In your present life, what are the things against which you bar the door? Sense the locked door in your heart and mind which is barred by fear. Who is shut out?

Now feel the presence of Jesus come into your heart and mind through that locked door. Feel his presence and the joy, the delight of being with him. Let him speak to you, "Peace."

He tells us that the sins we retain are retained, those we let go of are forgiven. Are there sins, offenses, fears, that we need to let go of?

Let the Spirit of God move through you if she will, releasing, letting go, encouraging, empowering. Feel the locked door melt away as fear is replaced by love, by the power of God. Sense yourself set free, empowered, sent by the Spirit of God.

As you are ready, close your meditation with a silent word of thanks, and bring yourself back into the presence of your group. For a few moments, share your feelings and insights in the group. How did it feel to be in the locked room with the disciples? How does it feel to move from fear to being empowered and sent? How does God's presence now help us move from fear to joy as a basis for our action in the world?

The groups have about fifteen minutes to share their reflections on the passage. Then, with the groups still in place, we take a few minutes for people to share with the total group insights or questions about what we have done so far in the workshop.

Resources for Community Study and Action (Unit 4)
(PW)

Both the Nuclear Storytelling and the Bible Study are effective for use in congregational settings as adult study group experiences. There are also a number of other ways to begin to address the issues, and numerous resources available. I would like to share a number of these with you, in the context of our three circles of action: the personal, the interpersonal and the transpersonal. First, let me give you a bit of background.

"We need a way of knowing that is capable of *forming* and *transforming* as well as *informing* people." This wonderful one-liner by religious educator Thomas Groome presents us with the tension that many of us as teachers and educators have felt. There has been a kind of dichotomy between the head and the heart, what Jim Fowler calls the "rational and passional" ways of knowing. Parker Palmer in his book, *To Know as We are Known: A Spirituality of Education*, says that "the truth we seek to know is a truth that also seeks to know us. The reality we pursue in study is not a collection of inert objects, "out there" and distant from us. Instead, it is a community of beings in continual quest of each other, an organic system of knowers and knowns yearning to renew their original communal relatedness." Too often when we attempt to do peace education we become fixated on the facts, the data, the "out there" and the abstract. We are given massive doses of information, but somehow we are not transformed by it. From our work in learning theory we are aware that rational thinking and data gathering are only one form of knowing, and that we must deal with other levels, those of feeling, story, community, as well as ideas and opinions. Thus, as we look at some of the resource material available to our congregations, let us return to our three circles of peacemaking as a context in which to look at "formation", "information," and "transformation."

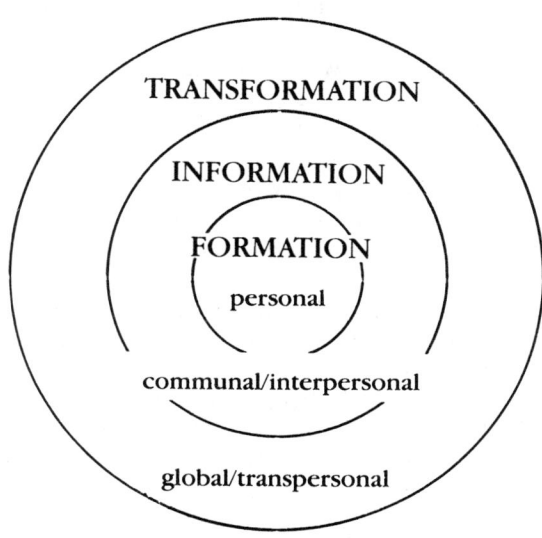

The first circle, which we called PERSONAL, is where the process of spiritual *formation* begins. As we attempt to become more centered, we "fill our wells" with spiritual food for the journey. Each of us has his/her favorite meditative practices and favorite readings. I will share only a few that have informed my journey. They are resources for putting myself back in focus. As Br. Wayne Teasdale has said, "To be out of focus essentially means to be uncentered, not to be in contact with the deepest level of reality and the profoundest aspiration of the heart.... Disorder in the soul and its relationship with the Source, with God, cannot but be reflected in society and its many problems, tensions and inequities."

Having engaged in reflection, we move to the other side of the balance, toward action. And action occurs first in community, in the INTERPERSONAL realm. There is a component of this middle range which does require *information* about the issues confronting us, in order to move us toward *transformation*.

Let me stress here that peace education needs to be done in a community context, a study group, an adult class, a prayer/care/

share group. We cannot be peacemakers without the support of others who share the journey; otherwise we run the risk of "burnout" and despair. I participated for two years in a Tuesday morning Peace Eucharist and breakfast which was a major source of "feeding" during the years that I commuted to Washington to work with the National Peace Academy Campaign as the public education person. Part of the feeding was the reading that we did in our worship/study together, and part of it was knowing that there was a community of fellow Christians who shared the journey.

It is in those small faith groups that we also are called to love constantly. I remember one encounter with my rector, late in the spring when we were both over-extended and verging on "burnout." He was requesting volunteers for some peace-related project and was frustrated that we all seemed to have reasons not to volunteer. He chastised us for not being willing to help on this project, and I exploded. (Beware of over-extended Pennsylvania Dutch grandmothers early in the morning!) I think we were both shocked, and it was out of that moment of anger and frustration that a deeper bonding grew. This is also an example of the need for picking your priorities. We can't do it all, and part of peace education is to assist us in discerning where our own personal gifts and graces lie.

"The distress of our choices is our chance to be blessed," says the poet W.H. Auden. Not everyone will be comfortable "acting" in an overtly political way such as petition drives, demonstrations, even writing members of congress. But some of these same people may well serve in a "Community Food Shelf" or soup kitchen, serving as peacemakers among the "least of these." And finally, as the Roman Catholic Bishops attest in their Pastoral letter on War and Peace, "people may agree in abhorring an injustice, for instance, yet sincerely disagree as to what practical approach will achieve justice. Religious groups are as entitled as others to their opinion in such cases, but they should not claim that their opinions are the only ones that people of good will may hold." (p. 282) Some of the peace education resource material is ideologically more radical than other material, and I have tried to note that in the bibliography. Be sensitive to the multiplicity of perspectives available, and remember as the Bishops note: "To teach the ways of peace is not to weaken the nation's will, but to be concerned about the nation's soul—we have only begun the journey toward a theology of peace; . . . we are confident that all the models of . . . education which have served the Church and our country so well in so many ways will creatively rise to the challenge of peace."(*The Challenge of Peace*, p. 304)

Peace Education resources hopefully will address our lives at all three levels—personal, interpersonal and transpersonal. To be educated, to know (knosis) requires us, as Parker Palmer suggests, to be "challenged to subject our lives to the Word in which we and the world were created. We sense danger in that challenge, because it requires that we stop relying on our own powers and throw ourselves upon a power beyond our own. But this is the "danger" to which Christian faith always calls us, the leap beyond that point where our knowledge claims certainty and gives us control, a leap into that place where we know ourselves to be known and loved by a Spirit who works not toward violence but toward the Peaceable Kingdom" (*To Know as We are Known*, Parker Palmer).

Let us now look at a few of the specific resources available:

At this point in the workshop, we walk behind the resource table, hold up and talk about some of the specific resources available for the work of peacemaking. The reader will find complete citations in the bibliography. Following here is a brief narrative description of some of the materials available.

Peacemaking Resources for the PERSONAL Journey:

A Testament of Devotion, Thomas Kelly

My copy of Kelly's book was originally a gift from my friend and mentor, Jim Fowler, who spoke of it as "a window I have found clear." As one who struggles with devotional writing, as perhaps a bit un-wordly, I am comforted by knowing that Kelly spent part of his life teaching at Earlham and the other part working with the American Friends Service Committee in Germany prior to the outbreak of World War II.

Despair and Personal Power in the Nuclear Age, Joanna Macy

This book is a guide to "despair" and "empowerment" work. Those terms refer to the psychological and spiritual work of dealing with our knowledge and feelings about the present planetary crisis in ways that release energy and vision for creative response. It is a workbook for dealing with the feeling level.

Our Many Selves, Elizabeth O'Conner

". . . it is intended that you be led into a dialogue with yourself which will lead to a new self-understanding, a continuing pattern of growth, and the creation of a new being in your life." This works well as an individual book or in a study group. I used it for several years in my "Shalom Woman" courses.

Reaching Out, Henri Nouwen

One reviewer noted, "This is essential reading and practical, well-balanced advice for those who wish to deepen their own spiritual life and practice of prayer." It was for me a new way of viewing Christian community, moving from hostility to hospitality.

Bringing Forth in Hope, Denise Priestly

"In setting out to write this book, I discovered a passage from Scripture which engaged my mind, my heart, my imagination; a passage which spoke to me of the struggle going on within me between hopelessness and hope. It is the symbol from Chapter 12 of the Book of Revelation: a woman gives birth while a dragon stands before her ready to devour her child. This symbol will serve to structure my examination of Christian hope."

Resources for the INTERPERSONAL and Community level

Family Resources

The Butter Battle Book, Dr. Seuss

This delightful yet thoughtful book tells of the escalating battle between the Yooks and the Zooks over whether to eat bread with the butter side up or down. The artillery escalates, the walls grow higher, and the book ends on the verge of the final confrontation with the ultimate weapon, "the big-boy boomeroo."

Fifty-Seven Reasons not to have a Nuclear War, Asher

This little carry-it-in-your-purse book is a series of pictures and captions celebrating life and creation. A wonderful antidote to doom and gloom.

Sadako and the Thousand Cranes, Eleanor Coerr

This is the classic story of a young Japanese girl dying of leukemia after the Atomic Bomb has been dropped on Japan. She believes that she will live as long as she continues to make paper cranes. It has inspired the various paper crane projects in churches and schools.

What about the Children?, Parents/Teachers for Social Responsibility

This is a good example of what a local community group can do to raise awareness and focus concerns on the school. For example, should parents sign permission slips for the use of pain-killing medications in the event of an attack during the school day?

*Parenting for Peace and Justice/
Educating for Peace and Justice*,
James and Kathleen McGinnis
    These are some of the best resources for parents and teachers, full of good common sense approaches and exercises. The McGinnises bring a deep personal commitment as well as professional expertise and I very highly recommend their work.

Peacemaking in the Family, Mr. Rogers
    Fred Rogers is also a Presbyterian minister, and he has combined his faith concern with his gift of reaching children in this very helpful resource.

Talking to our Children about Nuclear War, Van Ornum
    This is an attempt to move beyond "psychic numbing" and find ways to talk about both the hopes and the fears with our children. We know of their deep concerns, but we are often afraid to raise the issues. Hard work, but important.

Community Resources

Handbook for World Peacemaker Groups, Gordon Cosby, Bill Price
    "A world peacemaker group is a small gathering of people, who, conscious of the action of the Holy Spirit in their lives, offer the gift of their corporate life for the world's healing and unity through peacemaking. The Group has both an "inward" and "outward" journey. This is a useful resource for anyone wanting to build Christian community."

Building Christian Community—Pursuing Peace with Justice
    "This is a six-session guide for use in church settings....for persons seeking to combine Christian faith with active pursuit of peace with justice in our world ... and (who) recognize the need for Christian fellowship ... to face the unprecedented dangers we already know about, and to gain empowerment to accept the good news of our faith to meet this crisis." Each session combines work on the "inward" and the "outward" journey.

Peacemaking and the Community of Faith
    "This handbook is conceived as a guide for those who seek to bring their concern for peace and disarmament to local congregations ... it is intended to be a practical book; a book of suggestions and a compilation of ideas for worship, education and action by people and communities of faith." A fine introductory resource.

In addition to the above, many denominations have their own materials. I think that the Presbyterian Church materials are especially good. Titles include: "Dealing with Conflict in the Congregation," Peacemaking Through Worship Series, "The Things that Make for Peace." Also recommended in special settings is *Peace Futuring*, a resource developed by the United Church of Christ, which enables people to "vision" a bit about alternative futures. It has a workbook and teacher's guide. The Sojourners materials are excellent—with this caveat: they are radical in their approach to discipleship, and their language may be offensive to those who are not yet "converted." ("A Matter of Faith;" "Call to Conversion;" and "Waging Peace.")

Resources for the TRANSPERSONAL/JUSTICE level

It is at this level that I have included the activist materials, as well as some basic books for grounding in the public policy dimension. Much of the community concern "radiates" out to this level as well; thus the selection is somewhat arbitrary.

Center for Defense Information—Defense Monitor and Resource Packets, films

CDI is a group of career military men who have come to realize that the current policy decisions are bringing us closer to war, not adding to our security. These resources are fairly technical, but their films *The Arms Bazaar* and *War Without Winners* are excellent.

IMPACT

This is a mainline, ecumenical network for legislative information, citizen participation and grass roots action. It provides study reports (which we called "Prepares,"—to prepare constituents) and a monthly newsletter ("Update"), as well as legislative alerts (ACTION). Every congregation should have at least one subscription, and perhaps participate in state IMPACT networks.

Bread for the World

This grass roots lobby begun by Art Simon (brother of Senator Paul Simon, and himself a Lutheran minister), has worked for a number of years both to educate church members about the complexity of foreign aid and to influence food policy legislation. It is one of the "justice" lobbies that many church people are involved in and provides excellent training for grass roots organizing.

Several basic books which I also suggest are:

The Idea of Disarmament, Alan Geyer
 This is one of the best resource books on the Arms race, it's "Three Nuclear Ages," and the politics of disarmament. The chapter on "A Theology of Peacemaking" is superb. Alan Geyer, Director of the Center for Theology and Public Policy at Wesley Seminary, is probably the leading theological expert in this field. He is currently working with the United Methodist Church to produce their document on Peace.

Nuclear Holocaust and Christian Hope, Ronald Sider and Richard Taylor
 This is more overtly biblical-theological discussion than the Geyer book, and the section on Non-Military Defense is radical in its call.

What About the Russians: A Christian Approach to US/Soviet Conflict, Edited by Dale W. Brown
 Dale Brown teaches at Bethany Seminary and has pulled together a fine series of essays dealing with history, politics, culture, and faith. This is probably the most significant question in many churches, and thus beginning to break down some of the stereotypes and remove the "face of the enemy" is an act of stewardship in learning to love the enemy.

First Steps to Peace, The Fund for Peace
 This 1985 guide is a very useful listing of a variety of peace education resources, from basic books to films to speakers. It has a special section on resources for use with children as well as one on specific resources for clergy and congregations. It is a handy introduction to materials beyond those listed here.
 Many statements of denominations may be found in "To Proclaim Peace: Religious Communities Speak Out on the Arms Race," from the Fellowship of Reconciliation.

A final word about resources. My bias is clear in this section. If you browse bibliographies, you will be overwhelmed by the amount and diversity of material available. Let me simply reiterate my concern that education has the task of Formation, Information and Transformation. Much of the material that has been produced deals only with the Informational aspect. Be resourceful yourselves and use people resources as often as possible. Storytelling is still one of the best forms of education. Remember, too, the four levels of awareness—first, feelings, story, community; and only then ideas and opinions.

At this point in the workshop we break for lunch and allow participants an opportunity to browse through the resource material. Following lunch we continue to deal with the level of "Community" with some concrete resources and an exercise in conflict management. This provides a bridge between the levels of "Community" and "Ideas/Opinions" by providing some tools to deal with the diversity and range of opinions around these issues.

Conflict and Reconciliation (Unit 5)
(PW)

This morning we dealt with our own stories and part of the biblical story. We also looked at some of the resources available to us which might be used in each of our three circles of action. Let us now look at some of the very concrete ways in which we deal with conflict, once again on three levels.

Let us begin this discussion by taking a moment to look at our language. The field of Conflict Resolution got its name from Dr. Kenneth Boulding, the economist who with his wife Elise Boulding began one of the early centers for the study of Conflict at the University of Michigan. Kenneth recently commented to me that he wished he had chosen a different name, perhaps, "Conflict Management". The reality is that we never totally resolve conflict in the sense that we fix it and it goes away. Rather it is more like a dance where we learn not to step on each other's feet; we don't ever totally resolve the issues, but we do learn to manage the dance more gracefully.

Let's look at another language question: the names we use to speak about those persons or nations with whom we are in conflict. When we speak of the "evil empire" we convey a strong sense of the enemy which we must overcome. Elise Boulding has done a lot of work with Nongovernmental Organizations (NGO's) at the United Nations and she taught me something out of her own experience that speaks to our task as Christian peacemakers who are called to love our enemies. She said that if she could shift her language and use the word "stranger" rather than "enemy" that she found it also changed her mind-set. With a stranger there is always the possibility of moving from estrangement to reconciliation, whereas with an enemy there is by definition an adversarial relationship. I have been surprised how much difference it has made for me to look upon the "stranger" as a person from whom I can learn, who perhaps shares some portion of the truth, and with whom I can work to produce a reconciliation of our differences. This enables me to operate out of hope rather than fear.

Another example of how the "face of the enemy" changes with time can be found in some of the old propaganda posters and movies of the Second World War. They use much of the same language used currently to describe the Russians. In the 1940's that language was describing the Germans and the Japanese who are now our friends. The language remains constant, but the face of the enemy changes. This is not to say that we do not have legitimate and powerful disagreements with other persons and other ideologies. But there are emerging some new "paradigms" or models with which to deal with these conflicts, to keep that spiral of conflict from escalating to the level of violence.

At this point in the workshop, it might be helpful to look at our own perceptions of enemy. We tend to deny that we ourselves could have personal enemies, and yet we are often surprised to discover that there are persons whom we perceive as "other." The following exercise is one used by Diane Perlman.   *(see facing page)*

A New Paradigm

Roger Fisher of the Harvard Negotiation Project suggests that we need a new paradigm, that we have historically dealt with conflict in terms of win-lose. Competition between persons, teams and nations has been governed by the understanding that if one side wins, the other will of necessity lose. In a nuclear era with our increased understanding of the threat of a nuclear winter, we are operating with a new paradigm, that of lose-lose. Many of our leading scientists have shown us that "a nuclear war is not winnable." What Fisher is suggesting is that we need to evolve to the next level and begin to create models for win-win conflict styles. In his book *Getting to Yes* he describes this four-step process.

1. Separate the people from the problem

Let us take the case of a couple who wish to build a house. They have certain limitations, size of the lot, finances, and perhaps in some parts of the country, the weather. (Got to get the roof on before the snow!) They find that they can agree on certain basic designs but end up fighting over some of the specifics. Usually an architect (mediator) is called in to listen to the needs of both parties and to draw up a plan. In this way the couple focuses their energy on the plan rather than personalizing the problem. On a

Exercise on Enemy Imaging in Everyday Life

1. Think of someone with whom you are in conflict or whom you just dislike. This could be a boss, a coworker, a relative, an ex-spouse, or a president.
2. How do you feel when you think about this problem?
3. How much energy do you invest in putting this person down? How does that affect you?
4. How much do you enjoy getting agreement with your allies about how bad he/she is?
5. How much do you avoid or limit communication with this person?
6. To what extent does putting this person down make you feel good about yourself? How aware are you of all the ways in which you are better than him/her?
7. How uncomfortable do you feel if you get information about this person that contradicts your theory about him/her? If they've done something good, do you reinterpret their behavior? (For instance, they had ulterior motives, or did it because of someone else?)
8. How reluctant are you to change your opinion and let go of your dislike? What would you be giving up?
9. Right now, are you saying to yourself, "Yeah, sure, but they really are this way!"
10. Think of a time when you actually reconciled with someone. How uncomfortable was it at first? and afterward?
11. Think of a time when you forgave someone for something. How did it feel inside? Why is it so difficult to forgive?
12. Think of a time when someone had something against you, misunderstood you, misinterpreted your words or behavior, or just didn't understand your value system, personal history, or culture. How did you feel? Was it difficult to clear up the misunderstanding? What did you want them to know about you?
13. Think of a time when you apologized to someone. How difficult was it for you? What effect did it have on the other person? on the relationship? Why is it so difficult to apologize? What do you have to give up? What do you stand to gain?
14. Think of a time when you learned something new about someone that totally changed your understanding of them or of a particular situation. From *Changing the Image of the Enemy,* copyright by Diane Perlman, Ph.D., 1984, 617 Zollinger Way, Merion Station, PA 19066 (215-664-1654).

global level this plan or "single negotiating text" approach was used at Camp David, and it was Roger Fisher who designed that negotiating text. The use of the text enabled Sadat and Begin to work with a common plan rather than getting bogged down in the ideological issues between them. Gandhi once said that our task was to eliminate the antagonisms, not the antagonists.

2. Focus on interests, not positions
It is Fisher's contention that in any conflict there are certain common self interests. Church conflict expert Speed Leas speaks of common "needs." Fisher tells the story of two men arguing in a library. One wants the window open "to get some fresh air." The other wants it closed "to avoid the draft." Ultimately they find themselves locked into their positions, open versus closed. The librarian's solution is to open a window in an adjacent room which affords fresh air without creating a draft. In families many of us have learned through parent effectiveness training not to get locked into a win-lose position of having to be intransigent in our position just because we are the parent. Often in my house one of the areas of compromise is over bedtimes and curfews. I have learned that when I am arbitrary it escalates the conflict, but when we are able to "split the difference" that often works out well. I am sure that you have all had some experience akin to having one child cut the pie and the other choose the piece in order to make it "fair." These common ways of dealing with conflict create win-win situations without our remaining locked into static positions.

On a global level we witnessed the Russian willingness to return to the negotiating table after months of being locked into a position of saying that they would not return until the West pulled midrange missiles out of Europe. At some point they realized that it was in their self interest to return to the table and not remain locked in an untenable position.

Gandhi spoke of *satyagraha* or truth force, looking for the truth in each side's position. Inherent in this strategy is the understanding that each person shares some portion of the truth, something which Gandhi taught us in his political stance in India. Fisher, like Gandhi, suggests that the next step is to look for alternatives that meet some of the common self interests and reflect some of each person's portion of the truth.

3. Invent options for mutual gain
Fisher suggests a process akin to "brainstorming" to look at what I like to call the "100 possibilities." This is not the time to judge the practicality of the options but to get as many of them out on the

table as possible. Instead of assuming there is not enough food to go around, new ways of producing food were envisioned, such as the "Green Revolution," which introduced new agricultural technology into third world countries. Thus, in effect, more food was produced rather than having the "pie" cut in smaller pieces.

Another part of the process is similar to what Paulo Friere, Martin Luther King and Gandhi used and what has come to be called *conscientization* or Consciousness Raising. As we look at the problem, diagnose it, plan actions to try to alleviate or solve it, and finally reflect on those actions, we live out a rhythm of action/reflection which enables us to broaden our perspective and to look at our action steps critically. This leads to Fisher's fourth and final step.

4. Insist on using objective criteria
In global negotiations we often speak of verifiability. How do we know that "they" will play by the rules of the game that we have mutually established? In football there are referees, in baseball umpires. These folk are charged with making sure that there is some method of accountability built into the process. In family settings there is some clear understanding of what happens if a teenager stays out beyond curfew. Hopefully these consequences are mutually agreed upon.

The process of negotiation takes time and commitment. But, that cost can always be weighed against what Fisher speaks of as BATNA, which stands for "Best Alternative to a Negotiated Agreement." In any non-negotiated situation what are my options? What is the cost of not dealing with a conflict in a relationship or a congregation? What are the global options if we do not reach some sort of negotiated agreement on nuclear arms? What is the alternative if we choose not to attempt to love our enemies? What Fisher calls the moment of *getting to yes* is that point at which the parties feel that they have negotiated a workable agreement and in fact have reached a win-win solution.

Conflict Management Styles

I will now describe a few of the different conflict management styles out of which we deal with conflicts in various settings. These have been described by a member of the Alban Institute staff, Speed Leas, in his paper *Discover Your Conflict Management Style*. It might be helpful to consider using his instrument alone or with a group that you work with in a community or church setting. Leas suggests six basic strategies which we use to a greater or lesser degree, usually one or two most often. They are:

Persuade
This strategy usually works best in settings of mutual trust, and thus is not as useful in deeply conflictual situations, such as a divorce settlement where the level of trust is low and the level of anger/anxiety is high. Often in our efforts at peace education, we attempt to persuade other people that we are right. With low trust levels and high anxiety the negative outcomes of such persuasive efforts are predictable.

Compel
We all do this with small children when they run out into the street; and there are times when force is exercised legitimately between adults as well. But my criteria for that would be to ask whether the claims of justice are served by the use of force. The non-violent resistance of the civil rights movement which we see re-emerging in the demonstrations about apartheid in South Africa can be seen as a legitimate use of force. But because force can so often be misused, it must be limited to "critical moments."

Avoid/Accommodate
Many churches have what has been called a "no conflict norm." If the topic is controversial, avoid it. Very often, as we have seen, that makes it impossible to deal with issues such as peace and justice. But there are moments when we all avoid conflict. I attempt to do so at the dinner table since it becomes a lose-lose situation to fight at mealtimes. The food gets cold or goes uneaten, or, at worst, becomes a weapon. Whatever communion we hope for in the "breaking of bread" is shattered.

Another way to avoid conflict that I alluded to before is to outwait your teenagers. They will ultimately grow up and leave home! I remember a wonderful Monty Python movie in which the hero's favorite line was "Run away! Run Away!" Although initially we avoid the confrontation, and gain some peace, the likely outcome of this style is that the conflict is really not resolved, and it will probably come back to haunt us at a later moment.

Collaborate
Many of us who have been through the humanistic psychology movement or pastoral care courses in the past couple of decades are well aware that collaboration has been the style idealized by many of us in churches. It works well when persons are highly mo-

tivated, and have time to work through the issues involved. It works best in "both-and" settings, rather than those where only one option is possible—"either-or." Many of the mediation settings that Fisher describes are amenable to collaboration, as are many conflicts in our families and church communities. Appended is a list of resources that may be especially helpful to those of you wanting to work creatively on conflict management in the church. (Page 56)

Negotiate
Much of what we have discussed earlier with respect to Roger Fisher's work falls into this area. Speed Leas calls this style "bargaining," and I think it is often used in conjunction with collaboration.

Support
Finally, we come to the style used by many in support communities and helping environments. It is often seen as encouraging and enabling the person to resolve the conflict without stepping in to "fix it" for them. Empathic listening is a form of support, and much of what women have called "nurturing" is in this category. This leads me to one last distinction about conflict styles which Fisher and Leas do not address. It will be dealt with in some greater detail in the final chapter on the research findings, because we think it is a very important consideration. But let me just note it here.

Care And Justice—Attachment and Separation

Our research has shown that there are different modes of value construction that affect the lenses through which we view conflict. Leas speaks of it as an accommodating stance in which "a person ... often believes that the relationship is more important than the issue, and will therefore shrink from any confrontation that might be required to deal with the issue in order not to jeopardise the relationship." This choice has often been labeled as "feminine" and unfortunately seen as weakness. I would like to suggest that a conflict management style which values relationship, which takes seriously the requirements to love one's enemy, to love "constantly" as Micah would say, requires that we value relationship and community as much as we do rights and justice. To move back to our three circles for a moment, we must constantly be moving through all three levels/circles and constantly be expanding our understanding of community and relationship. We must, if we are to survive, live out of hope rather than fear, out of reconciliation rather than estrangement, out of win-win rather than lose-lose.

At this point in the workshop, participants are asked to stand up, move into an open area of the building, and join in an exercise in conflict management called Crossing the Line.

The group is divided into sets of partners, preferably male/female if possible. Each team is given a strip of masking tape and asked to create a line between them, with each person positioned on opposite sides of the line. The task is to "persuade" one's partner to cross the line. This must be done non-verbally and three minutes are given to "resolve the conflict." Note that the key to the success of this exercise is the manner in which the instructions are given, because the task must be defined in an open-ended way.

A number of styles emerge in this exercise. Often one person will attempt to persuade *another (frequently with bribes and manipulation) to cross the line. Sometimes there will be a show of* force *as one person attempts to pull the other over the line. (Coercion may also be exercised by one who simply refuses to yield, leaving the other to solve the problem.) One partner may walk away and avoid the conflict, whereas another will cross over simply to* accommodate *"rather than fight about it." Collaboration is seen when each partner changes sides, or when the line is straddled. There is often a period of* negotiation *before that takes place. The body language can reveal whether the partners have been able to* support *each other in the process or whether one or the other feels that he or she has "lost." One of the most creative solutions is simply to remove the line, by picking up the tape. All lines are to a greater or lesser degree arbitrary!*

In the debriefing of this exercise people have a chance to share their own conflict management style and it is a good opportunity for some laughter and a shift of mood.

The material on conflict management helps create a context in which "Ideas and Opinions" can be discussed. We continue with this level of awareness in the next section in which the rationale for the various activities of the day is shared with the participants. Most of that material on the "levels of awareness" has been shared with the reader in chapter one, and is not repeated here.

Planning for Peace in the Parish (Unit 6)
(RTG)

In this final section of the workshop, I would like to do two things. First, I would like to suggest that peacemaking in a congregational setting has some unique aspects. Second, I would like to share with you some of the developmental theory which undergirds the various activities we have used throughout the day.

Planning for *peace in the parish* is unlike other planning in at least two ways. First, a parish or congregation is more like a family than like a business, union, or political party in which we might set an objective and mobilize everyone to reach it. Groups within a congregation may take action, but it is unlikely that the congregation as a whole will agree. Congregations make poor "front line units" in the struggle for social change, but can support a number of individuals and groups in their involvements.

Second, planning for *peace* in the parish is different from other planning because peace is not an objective or program that we can accomplish this year or the next. It is not the responsibility of one group within the congregation. Our concern needs to be long-term, perhaps lifelong. We cannot "do" peace and move on to something else. Peace is a way of life that needs to inform all our doing, and all of our activities in the parish.

In the workshop, there follows here a discussion of infusing peacemaking concerns in congregational life, with an explanation of the "levels of awareness" presented in Chapter 1 of this book.

All of the tools we have used in the workshop, you can use in your congregation. Having looked at the various levels of awareness on which you need to approach any issue in the congregation, I'd like to leave with you four specific points:

1) Use the resources of your denomination.

If a statement on the issue has been made by some group within your denomination, it is always appropriate to say, "Well, we may not agree with these people but we ought to find out what they have to say because they're our folks."

Further, if you can find historical precedents in the actions or statements of your denomination, it's even better. The principle is "We⎯⎯⎯⎯⎯⎯⎯have always...." The early Abolitionists turned to the past, reviving the motto on the great cracked bell in Philadelphia to say, "We Americans have always been a people called 'To Proclaim Liberty to All the Land.'" It was from them that it got the name "The Liberty Bell."

2) Build small groups.

People need face to face interaction; small groups can best support the expression of feelings about the issues; various different small groups can meet the needs and interests of a variety of people; and small groups can offer "anti-burnout" support to those engaged in long-term issues and ministries. The materials from World Peacemakers coming out of the Church of the Savior are particularly good in articulating the balance between the inward and outward journeys as we deal with issues. Also the materials on peacemaking in the community of faith from the Fellowship of Reconciliation are particularly useful because of that organization's long history, ecumenical scope, and global connections. The "peace fellowships" within your own denominations may be able to provide linkages and personal support beyond the local congregation.

3) Give people something concrete to do.

The "social issue" that people are most involved in is probably hunger, in part because working in a soup kitchen, bringing canned goods to church, fasting or walking for a day to raise money for famine relief are tangible things that people can do. One good source of inspiration and handouts is The Christophers, who offer stories and suggestions built on the theme that "It is better to light one candle than to curse the darkness." A peace packet is available.

4) Act within the system.

Those of you who are called to make a prophetic or radical witness are probably already doing so. Almost by definition, the great majority of people (of us) are going to be conventional. Those of us who are conventional tend to support the system, we respect credentialed authority, and we're proud to be Americans. Thus "mainline/mainstream" resources work best—those like materials from

The Churches Center for Theology and Public Policy at Wesley Seminary, the Center for Defense Information with its staff of former career military officers, and the IMPACT network run by the Washington-based staff of the mainline denominations.

In a moment, I am going to ask you to think about how you can use some of what you have learned in this workshop in your own congregation. I hope that what we have done will help you so that "peace" does not become a divisive issue in your congregation. Probably most people in your congregation are "for peace." Some might identify themselves as "peacemakers," others might think of themselves more as "peacekeepers." Both keeping the peace and making peace can be good activities in the personal, interpersonal and transpersonal spheres of action. Both can also become coercive, "keeping the lid on," forcing "reconciliation" on those who are not ready, perpetuating oppression or injustice. None of us have cornered the market on peace. Differences will continue, not least of all between "peacemakers" and "peacekeepers" within our congregations; but within the Christian tradition we say that "Christ is our peace who has broken down the middle wall of separation between us." As the poet W.H. Auden says in "For the Time Being," "Therefore at every moment we pray that, following Him, we may depart from our anxiety into His Peace."

Participants give a short evaluation of the day and briefly plan their next steps for action. There follows a short presentation on peacemaking in worship and a closing service.

Peacemaking in Worship (Unit 7)
(RTG)

Confession is an act of worship, and I approach the theme of peacemaking in worship with a personal confession. Years ago, as a young college chaplain, I perpetrated a number of what we then called "hard-hitting liturgies." It was only in time that I realized that I was promoting discord rather than peace. Out of that experience and others, I offer a few thoughts about peacemaking in worship.

Worship is not a forum in which we change people's minds. At best, we bring the concerns of life and allow the Spirit to work on our hearts. We need to promote openness of heart and mind, rather than closing them with our judgments and "hard-hitting" words. If we are open to hear, the words of scripture themselves are "like a hammer that breaketh the rock in pieces."

Truth must be spoken, but it must be spoken in love. Research and common observation tell us that people are more open to hearing "social action" sermons from pastors whom they perceive care about them. Good pastoral work is the foundation of prophetic ministry in congregations. Further, the truth spoken must be more than current opinion. All political conclusions are flawed by sin and stand under judgment; the Bible seldom provides "an answer" to a specific policy issue. The source of specific facts and opinions should be clearly given when other than biblical material is used in sermons. People are seldom converted to a point of view by one sermon, however good it is, but a sermon which admits of more than one conclusion can have the powerful effect of "giving permission" to talk about a difficult topic in a congregation.

People bring different expectations to worship than they bring to an educational or political forum. In church, people are more receptive, less individually critical, more willing to be dependent, more open to the leading of a spirit. This is as it should be when we consciously attempt to open ourselves to God's presence, and we need to be careful that we do not violate that vulnerability. By way of negative example, some confessions about social issues written for corporate use put words in people's mouths to which they have not consciously consented. People may participate in such corporate expressions and then subsequently feel manipulated and angry.

Whenever possible, use familiar forms and worship resources. Most churches already have hymns, prayers, and other expressions which speak of peace, poverty, our common humanity, care for the created order and other social themes. These familiar forms can be used creatively, and innovations are most easily first introduced gradually outside of the main weekly service of the congregation. For example, one congregation began a weekly service for peace with a handful of participants. In time the small group of worshippers grew, began collecting food for the needy, and experimented with non-sexist language in their worship. Now many of these concerns have found their way into the mainstream of congregational life in that place.

It is always appropriate for people to express their deepest concerns in the context of prayer, and social concerns are appropriately shared in corporate prayer. In congregations where the pastor appears oblivious to peace and justice concerns, lay people may well say to him or her, "I'm really concerned about . . ., would you please remember this in our prayers." In congregations where people spontaneously offer prayers during worship it is important to set a climate in which a diversity of concerns may be offered so that the church does not become just one political party at prayer. Thus we may pray for both those who for conscience sake refuse military service, and the members of the armed forces; for victims of oppression on the right and on the left; etc.

Worship should allow us to bring the totality of who we are with all of life consciously into God's transforming presence. We bring many concerns that we also deal with in the political arena. However, worship allows us to deal with these concerns with a mind-set other than decision-making. Worship allows us to bring our convictions and uncertainties, our hurts and hopes and failings, and lay them before the transforming presence of the holy Other. In this we may discover metanoia—a change of heart, a change of mind, a change of direction. We may find ourselves accepted, healed, forgiven and empowered with new hope and vision for action.

The workshop closes with worship, using resources from the various traditions represented by the participants.

PART III—The Learnings

Participant Evaluations
(RTG)

At the close of the workshops, we ask the participants to write down both what was most valuable to them from the workshop and what one next step they plan to take. The data from these evaluations have provided the basis for our drawing some conclusions about the workshop model which are presented below.

As is often true with workshops, what was most helpful for many participants was the sense of support and hope gained through meeting with people from other churches who shared common concerns. The groups we worked with included both people who had been "activists" for some time and others who had not before publicly expressed their concerns. However, the design permitted an equality of participation from "newcomers" and those who were quite knowledgeable about the issues. Both groups mentioned the value of the networking and support aspects of the workshops, while the resources we provided were of importance primarily to those who were not so knowledgeable. Significantly, several who were long-time activists noted important learnings for themselves in the areas of personal sharing, spiritual grounding of the issues, movement from fear to hope as a basis for action, and emphasis on non-confrontational techniques. One clergywoman said, "The emphasis on ways to resolve conflicts, ways to listen to the 'warriors' and not antagonize them, were important to me because I tend to be confrontational." A clergyman in a congregation with many military personnel wrote on his follow-up survey that as a result of the workshop he felt, "an increased awareness of being able to reach anyone on this issue and accept where they are."

The positive tone and style of the day was frequently mentioned as important. We tried to model a non-confrontational style and avoid language which would seem to exclude persons on the basis of denomination, theological position, political stance, profession, sex, or age. There has been little negative feedback in this area and many evaluations commented on the feeling of inclusiveness. Every workshop has included a few people with initially negative perceptions of "peacemaking" activities in churches. Certainly not all have been "converted," but for these persons also, the workshop appears to have been positive. For example, one man who feels nuclear war unlikely and moral decay a greater threat said that he learned that some people in his congregation are genuinely troubled by the possibility of nuclear destruction. Another strongly committed to peaceful uses of atomic energy said he found that peace activists are not necessarily a threat to his position.

As part of the follow-up evaluation, participants were asked to rank order a list of 18 values. As might be expected from a survey in this context, participants were much more likely than the general American public to rate "A world at peace" a number one value. However, this ranking accounted for only 37% of the sample. "Salvation" was ranked first by 20%, "Inner harmony" chosen by 10%, and 17% picked other values including "freedom," "family," "self-respect," "mature love" and "an exciting life." The sample is too small to do further analysis, but it offers one more piece of evidence that we need to be sensitive to a range of different motivations. Further comparisons with the general American public suggest that "peacemakers" may be more inner-directed than those not already involved.

Evaluations submitted at the workshops and the follow-up survey of participants bear out the theory that different approaches work best for different people. Each section of the workshop was named as "most helpful" by at least five percent of participants. Most frequently mentioned as helpful were the conflict resolution materials and the "nuclear story telling." While the conflict resolution materials were rated most highly on the day of the workshop, in the retrospective survey, the "softer" nuclear stories and Bible study gained in value. Resources were seldom seen as the most valuable part of the day, but they were frequently asked for.

The few negative comments received were primarily about details at some of the early workshops. We learned to have a printed list of resources available, and to keep the working groups small. Groups of three for the nuclear stories and groups of six for the Biblical reflection seem about right in this context.

While not encouraging divisiveness, we did create some distinctions among participants for the purpose of analysis. We were particularly interested in the possibility that men and women or clergy and lay people might bring different styles to peacemaking activities and have different needs. The data we collected are presented in those categories below and the implications are discussed in the following chapter.

Male/Female differences—"Next steps"

At the end of each workshop, participants were asked to reflect for a few moments, and then write on a card what one *next step* they might commit themselves to as a result of their learnings from the day. We asked participants to indicate on the card their sex and "status" if they were ordained or a church professional. The following analysis was done on two random samples of cards from lay people. Each sample was drawn from all the workshops, excluding only cards which were not coded. Analysis was done by marking verbs and sorting on the basis of the type of activity indicated.

Twenty percent of both men and women indicated a first step which may be regarded as initially private or "internal," although it might be referenced to others. Expressions used by this group include: "sort out where I am; keep an open mind; change attitude; center; pray; shift focus; etc."

A further 28% of the men but only 8% of the women plan to "read, study, or consider" some material as a next step.

An equal 15% of both men and women plan some specific action or program with resource material, using verbs such as "buy, use, work, formulate, identify."

The largest percentage of both groups plan actions directly involving other people in interactive ways using verbs such as "talk, share, encourage, become involved, gather people." However, such direct action with others is contemplated as a next step by 35% of the men and 53% of the women. In these activities the men more frequently use verbs such as "gather, get, talk, start, lobby, involve" while women more frequently use verbs such as "help, share, link, listen." Further, in the overall analysis, only 8% of the men but 18% of the women modify their intended action with words such as "try, attempt, hope to. . . ."

Male/Female differences—"Most helpful"

Evaluation cards collected at the end of the workshop were coded and analyzed as described above. Statements of what was "most helpful" from the day fell into six categories: three of the six name specific elements of the workshop; sharing the "nuclear stories" in small groups; the Bible study; and the presentation on conflict management. The other three categories are more general, including:

references to the experience of being with others from various backgrounds who share common concerns, the value of the resources and theoretical base presented, and general comments about the emotional tone of the day and gains in personal insight and hopefulness. We refer to these six categories in shorthand as NUCLEAR STORIES, BIBLE STUDY, CONFLICT TOOLS, BEING WITH OTHERS, RESOURCES & THEORY, and GENERAL.

The general comments form the largest single percentage for both groups (38% women, 33% men); 18% of both groups describe being with others as the most helpful experience of the day.

Nuclear stories and conflict tools are the most frequently mentioned specific items for all respondents. Men are slightly more likely to rate nuclear stories as most helpful, but women are *twice* as likely to rate the conflict tools as most helpful (20% women *vs* 10% men).Men are twice as likely to note the resources and theory as most helpful (25% men, 12.5% women).

Clergy & lay differences

On the average, less than one-third of the participants in these workshops were ordained clergy or persons in religious orders. There has been little clergy/lay distinction in the course of the workshops since most of the activities such as "nuclear story telling" and "crossing the line" can be engaged in by all on an equal footing. In fact there is a remarkable similarity in the ratings given by clergy and lay people as to what was most helpful in the workshop. There are only two major differences. The laity more frequently than clergy commented on the value of being together with people of different traditions to discuss the subject, and the clergy mentioned the value of the framework and resources almost twice as frequently as lay people did. It seems reasonable to assume that clergy interested in the subject have more opportunities to meet with others, but place greater value on tools and resources because of their professional responsibilities.

The Feminine in Peacemaking
(PW)

Some of the research findings of this project as well as interviews with others involved in peacemaking activities suggest that there are two distinct modes of moral reasoning, as seen in the responses of men and women. Carol Gilligan in her book *In a Different Voice* describes these styles as the ethic of *Justice* and the ethic of *Care*. In earlier work, Robert May used the language of Pride and Care. (Developmental psychologists like Erik Erickson and educational psychologists like Lawrence Kohlberg have posited stages of development in which separation/individuation was perceived to be a more "mature" stage than the attachment/relationship stages. However, the work of Gilligan clearly shows that this is not necessarily a matter of higher/lower stage development, but rather a gender difference.) Since I have spent several years working with women in a variety of peacemaking/peace education situations, I am aware that there is an intuitive sense that these differences are real. Therefore, I wanted to see whether there was a link between the ways in which men and women differ in moral decision making and the ways they attended to peacemaking activities. Let me summarize my findings by describing three differences that I believe affect the way in which women deal with peace issues.

I call these three differences the three "C"s; community (relationship), context and concreteness. I will illustrate each of these and suggest why they are important to the task of designing peace education models/resources. First, women tend to be more communal and relational in their orientation. Carol Gilligan says "Women not only define themselves in the context of human relationship, but also judge themselves in terms of their ability to care." Nell Noddings, a professor of education at Stanford, has written a book called *Caring: A feminine approach to ethics and moral education*. One of her most significant statements is: "An important difference between an ethic of caring and other ethics . . . is its foundation in relation. The philosopher who begins with a supremely free consciousness—an aloneness and emptiness at the heart of existence—identifies ANGUISH as the basic human affect. But our view, rooted as it is in relation, identifies JOY as the basic human affect. It is the recognition of and longing for relatedness that form the foundation of our ethic, and the joy that accompanies fulfillment of our caring enhances our commitment to the ethical ideal that sustains us as one's caring." Ann Howard interviewed a number of the staff at WAND, (Women's Action for Nuclear Disarmament) and found that, "In describing their reasons for being involved with the issue, the first words from each person interviewed at WAND referred not to the devastation that would be wrought in a nuclear war, nor to the current waste of federal monies, but what they cared about saving and nurturing. . . . I found that the answers to these questions reflected a deep love of living relationships . . . to children, grandparents, the earth, to friends and even strangers. The answers gave an acute, often painful awareness of the preciousness of life, and what it is to care for and love someone. To speak of what is precious, what is dear, is not to speak of disembodied ideals such as freedom, honor, duty, but of concrete, tangible relationships." In our workshop evaluations, women more often than men used caring/relational language such as "help," "share," "listen," and planned next steps involving others. This is the language of nurture and support. Thus the first "C" is a sense that peacemaking happens in *community* and relationship.

The second "C" closely related is that of context. The root for this word is the word "contexere" which means to weave together. Very often women speak of their work in terms of weaving and webs. Joanna Macy, author of *Despair and Personal Power in a Nuclear Age*, makes much of the "web of life." Some of you may recall a women's demonstration several years back in which women spun webs linking one to another as a symbol of their interrelatedness. "The Ribbon Project" is a wonderful example of this contextual way of "making" peace. Speaking of Gilligan's work, Dorothy Austin, head of the Nuclear Education Project at Harvard Medical school, says: "No longer is woman's style of moral reasoning and the desire to preserve context perceived as less developed. It has become a political necessity for the preservation of the world." Another way to describe this yearning for context is to think in terms of a holistic approach rather than separating out the many distinct issues. As Parker Palmer suggests: "As women articulate their way of being in the world, we learn that our objectifying, analytic ways tend to reflect the male mode of experience. The female way of knowing is more connective, integrative, holistic, inclined to emphasize the relationships between things more than their distinctions." (53% of our sample of women spoke of their peace work in interactive, relational language).

Thus women ask more often how one piece is related, connected to another. This leads directly into the third "C": *concreteness*. This distinction between the "abstract" and the concrete is summed up in Nell Nodding's description of women's response to the hypothetical moral dilemmas used in Lawrence Kohlberg's research. "Faced with a hypothetical moral dilemma, women often ask for more information. It is not the case, certainly, that women cannot arrange principles hierarchically and derive conclusions logically. It is more likely that they see this process as peripheral or even irrelevant to moral conduct. They want more information, I think, in order to form a picture. Ideally, they need to talk to the participants to see their eyes and facial expressions, to size up the whole situation. Moral decisions, after all, are made in situations. They are qualitatively different from the solution of geometry problems. Women . . . give reasons for their acts, but the reasons point to feelings, needs, situational conditions, and their sense of personal ideal rather than universal principles and their application." (p. 96)

In church activities for social justice, women seem more comfortable dealing with concrete situations involving real people, whether that is an exchange with Soviet citizens, staffing a food closet, or providing sanctuary for a Latin American refugee family. Since women tend to live more in a relational mode, our evaluations showed that men were especially moved by the nuclear story telling. We suspect that this is because the story telling mode was new to them, while women are natural story tellers. Women, on the other hand, were excited by the concrete techniques of conflict management used to solve conflicts in family, church and community. The conflict management material gave them new tools to use in the contexts in which they most often work.

This is not to suggest that the more abstract concerns for justice should be downplayed. It is interesting to note that more and more of the writing and speaking about these concerns is couched in the language of "solidarity," to be in community/communion with our brothers and sisters who are oppressed. This humanizing language, using concrete examples of persons in specific contexts, brings peacemaking into the realm of "doing justice" rather than discussions "about justice."

I want to conclude with Gilligan's synthesis of the two modes. "To understand how the tension between responsibilities and rights (Care and Justice) sustains the dialectic of human development is to see the integrity of two disparate modes of experience that are in the end connected. While an ethic of justice proceeds on the premise of equality—that everyone should be treated the same—an ethic of care rests on the premise of nonviolence—that no one should be hurt. In the representation of maturity, both perspectives converge in the realization that just as inequality adversely affects both parties in an unequal relationship, so too violence is destructive for everyone involved." (p.174)

Understanding that there are two ways of perceiving the work of peacemaking, two ways of looking at the world, expands and enriches the peacemaking possibilities in our personal and congregational lives. For too long we have dealt with peacemaking in individualistic, impersonal and abstract terms. The gifts of the communal, contextual and concrete ways of peacemaking create a new wholeness to our work. My hope for this integrated style is that it will open us to go forth in new ways to love and serve God's people.

When we work with congregations to educate for peace, we must be attentive to differences, lest the divisions begin even before the content is presented. Let us be aware and celebrate the different sets of lenses, and honor both.

Reflections
(RTG)

It has not been the intent of this workshop to pretend that there are no political differences in regard to national policy issues, nor do we want to say that religion should never exercise a prophetic role which might call particular policies into question. However, we do see the role of the local church as far greater than informing people about issues or persuading them to adopt certain positions. Following the analysis of Bruce Reed of the Grubb Institute in *The Task of the Church and the Role of its Members*, we understand the congregation to be a place where more than rational discourse takes place. The church is a place where people can acknowledge their human limitations and be empowered to act with grace and courage. Potentially destructive or enervating feelings of dependence find their proper object in God, and the power of the transcendent is internalized so that people experience themselves as competent actors in the world. In order for this transforming action to take place, people need to be able to express their hopes and fears and allow themselves to be acted on in non-rational ways. Dealing with issues simply in terms of facts and imperatives to action may continue the discursive, rational process and our reliance on "human action" rather than allow the primary "religious process" to work. In Biblical terms, "being anxious," "trusting in princes," or "trusting in ourselves," prevents us from experiencing the power of God.

The threat of nuclear war, however remote the possibility, confronts us with an extreme case of human limitation. Our survival, the survival of everything we care about, any future we can imagine, seems threatened by forces over which we have no control. As mentioned earlier, Robert Jay Lifton and others have noted that many people cannot tolerate the threat of annihilation inherent in the existence of nuclear weapons and their own sense of powerlessness in the face of that threat; therefore, they restrict their awareness and participation in the world in many ways—they "don't think about it," or dismiss the threat lightly while diminishing their awareness of the world, the phenomenon called "psychic numbing." One form of this that we may see in churches is the escapist belief that "God will fix it," a belief which removes human responsibility and complicity in a real threat which humans have created.

To an outside observer, it would be clear that the existence of nuclear weapons determines the allocation of a major portion of the planet's resources, stymies the best minds, and makes the future of every human enterprise contingent upon their non-use. For all of us, the nuclear threat is a major form of the "shadow of death." When churches don't provide ways for people to deal with this threat, they are avoiding not only a social issue, but a major spiritual issue. Many people have found that facing into their nuclear fears has made them more open to the power of God in their lives and more aware of the delights of the creation. But we need to approach this journey into the shadow carefully. Because the threat is so overwhelming and so often denied it needs to be approached gently and in a supportive context. Many in the psychological disciplines suggest it is dangerous to destroy people's defenses before they are ready to give them up. Deep respect for persons, which comes from the Judeao-Christian tradition, may mean that we have no right to change another person. However, we can offer them both support and the possibility of visioning new options. Frequently the "secular" peace movements seem to appeal to the terror as a means of motivating people. We suspect that the long-range results of this approach are counter-productive. The churches have a great gift to offer society in helping people move from fear to hope as a basis for action.

"What would you like to have happen in your congregation around the issue of peace?" "What are you afraid may happen?" We have asked those questions of several hundred clergy and laypeople attending these workshops on "Peacemaking without Division." The fears stand out most clearly: most frequently the fear of polarization and anger, or for activists, the fear that apathy will dominate, that "nothing will happen." When we raise the nuclear issue, we touch all the energy of fear and helplessness that lies behind our silence. Further, many congregations have no way to deal with the expression of any disagreement or strong emotion. It is no wonder that those who might talk about issues of war and peace in their congregation fear that they might be greeted with anger, hostility and divisiveness—or fear that their efforts might be met with apathy and inaction, results which would increase their own feelings of powerlessness. The techniques we have explored in these workshops seem to offer ways to begin approaching the religious issues behind the "social issues" in ways that do not immediately trigger reactions of fear, hostility and polarization. We have attempted this first through the nuclear issue because it is so clearly an issue which touches every life, but we suspect that the anger or apathy around other social issues is similarly fed by more-than-rational human reactions which may defy discussion but cry out for expression in the religious context.

REFERENCES AND FURTHER RESOURCES

PART I

CHAPTER ONE: Developmental materials

Erikson, Erik H. *Childhood and Society*. W. W. Norton & Co. 1963.
Fowler, James. *Stages of Faith*. Harper and Row. 1981.
Fowler, James. *Becoming Adult, Becoming Christian*. Harper and Row. 1984.
Fowler, Jim and Keen, Sam. 1978. *Life Maps* Waco, TX: Word Books.
Kegan, Robert. *The Evolving Self*. Cambridge, MA: Harvard University Press. 1982.
Levinson, Daniel J. *The Seasons of A Man's Life* New York: Alfred A. Knopf. 1978.
Loevinger, Jane. *Ego Development* San Francisco: Jossey-Bass Publishers. 1977.
Perry, William G. Jr. *Forms of Intellectual and Ethical Development in the College Years*. New York: Holt, Rinehart and Winston. 1970.
Sheehy, Gail. *Passages*. New York: E. P. Dutton. 1974.
Wilcox, Mary. *Developmental Journey*. Nashville: Abingdon. 1979.

CHAPTER TWO: (citations)

Palmer, Parker. *To Know as We are Known*. New York: Harper and Row. 1983.
Simon, Arthur. *Bread for the World*. Paulist Press. 1975.

PART II
Works cited or referenced in text.
LISTED BY TITLE IN ORDER CITED

The Broken Connection, Robert J. Lifton. Simon and Schuster. 1979.
First Steps to Peace, The Fund For Peace, Suite 207M, 345 East 46th Street, New York, NY 10017. (single copies $2.60 plus $0.90 postage)
"Religious Education for Justice by Educating Justly," Thomas H. Groome in *Education for Peace and Justice* Edited by Padraic O'Hare Harper & Row. 1983.
"Contemplation and Responsibility" by Br. Wayne Teasdale in *Spiritual Life* (pages 31-34).
For The Time Being, W. H. Auden. Faber & Faber. London. 1945.
The Challenge of Peace. Bishops Peace Pastoral. National Conference of Catholic Bishops, Washington, DC.
To Know as We are Known, Parker Palmer. Harper and Row. New York, 1983.
Getting to Yes: Negotiating Agreement without Giving In, Roger Fisher and William Ury. Penguin Books. (paperback) 1983.
A Testament of Devotion, Thomas Kelly. Harper and Row, New York. 1941.

Despair and Personal Power in the Nuclear Age, Joanna Rodgers Macy. $8.95. New Society Publishers, 4722 Baltimore Ave, Philadelphia PA 19143. 1983.
Our Many Selves, Elizabeth O'Connor. Harper and Row, New York. 1971.
Reaching Out, Henri Nouwen. Doubleday, New York. 1975.
Bringing Forth in Hope, Denise Priestly. Orbis, Maryknoll, NY 1983.
The Butter Battle Book, Dr. Seuss. Random House, New York 1984.
Fifty Seven Reasons not to have a Nuclear War, Marty Asher. Warner Books, New York, 1984.
Sadako and the Thousand Cranes, Eleanor Coerr. Dell/Yearling, New York, 1977.
What about the Children?, Parents/Teachers for Social Responsibility, Box 517, Moretown, VT 05660.
Parenting for Peace and Justice/Educating for Peace and Justice, James and Kathleen McGinnis. Orbis, Maryknoll, NY. 1981.
Peacemaking in the Family, Mr. Rogers. Presbyterian Peacemaking Program, 475 Riverside Drive, New York, NY 10115.
Talking to our Children about Nuclear War, William and Mary Van Ornum. Continuum, New York. 1984.
Handbook for World Peacemaker Groups, Gordon Cosby, Bill Price World Peacemakers, 2852 Ontario Road, NW, Washington DC 20009.
Building Christian Community—Pursuing Peace with Justice, World Peacemakers, 2852 Ontario Road, NW, Washington DC 20009.
Peacemaking and the Community of Faith; Fellowship of Reconciliation, Box 271, Nyack, NY 10960.
The Idea of Disarmament, Alan Geyer, The Brethren Press, 1451 Dundee Ave, Elgin IL 60120.
Nuclear Holocaust and Christian Hope, Ronald Sider and Richard Taylor, 1982 Intervarsity Press, Downers Grove, IL.
What About the Russians: A Christian Approach to US/Soviet Conflict, Edited by Dale W. Brown. Brethren Press, 1451 Dundee Ave, Elgin, IL 60120.

Conflict Resources:

The Things That Make for Peace . . . Begin with Children, a four-session course for children, with two sessions on conflict management. $0.50 (PDS - see below)
Dealing With Conflict, a six-session course for congregations. $0.75 (PDS—see below)
Peacemaking in the Family, by Mister Rodgers. $0.50 (PDS)

PDS note: The three items above are available from the Presbyterian Distribution Service, 905 Interchurch Center, 475 Riverside Drive, New York, New York. 10017

Moving Your Church Through Conflict, Speed Leas, The Alban Institute, 4125 Nebraska Ave, Washington DC 20016.
Discover Your Conflict Management Style, Speed Leas. The Alban Institute, 4125 Nebraska Ave, Washington DC 20016.

GROUPS MENTIONED IN TEXT
(Alphabetical order)

Bread For The World, Citizen Action Network. 32 Union Square East. New York, NY 10003. (212) 260-7000.
Fellowship of Reconciliation, Box 271, Nyack, NY 10960.
IMPACT, 100 Maryland Avenue, NE, Washington DC 20002.
Leaven, 1320 Fenwick Lane, #500, Silver Spring, MD 20910. (301) 587-6310.
Peacelinks, 723 1/2 Eighth Street SE, Washington DC 20003. (202) 544-0805.

Sojourners, PO Box 29272, Washington, DC 20017

The Center for Defense Information, CDI, 600 Maryland Avenue SW, 303 Capitol Gallery West, Washington DC 20024. (202) 484-9490.

The Churches' Center for Theology and Public Policy, 4500 Massachusetts Avenue NW, Washington DC 20016. (202) 885-9100.

World Peacemakers, 2852 Ontario Road NW, Washington DC 20009. (202) 265-7582.

OTHER RESOURCES FOR FURTHER CONGREGATIONAL ACTION

Suggested for further study:

The Idea of Disarmament: Rethinking the Unthinkable by Alan Geyer. The Brethren Press. 1982.

The Nuclear Delusion: Soviet-American Relations in the Atomic Age by George Kennan. Pantheon Press. 1983.

Together on the Way The story of the Dialogue between the Churches of the United States and the Soviet Union. $2 copy from the US-USSR Church Relations Committee, Room 880, 475 Riverside Drive, New York, NY 10115.

Nuclear Ethics: A Christian Moral Argument by David Hollenbach, SJ, Paulist Press. $3.95 (paperback) 1982.

Educational Resources:

"Alternatives to Violence": A manual and course by Kathy Bickmore available from The Alternatives to Violence Committee, Cleveland Friends Meeting, 10916 Magnolia Drive, Cleveland OH 44106. $6.95 + $1 postage & handling.

"Peace Futuring", is a six-session course designed to explore future visions, available from the Office for Church in Society, the United Church of Christ, 105 Madison Avenue, New York, NY 10016.

"Peacemaking and the Community of Faith: A Handbook for Congregations" includes suggestions for worship, education, and action. $3 from the Fellowship of Reconciliation, Box 271, Nyack, NY 10960. (914) 358-4601.

"Peacemaking in Your Neighborhood" Jennifer E. Beer. New Society Publishers 4722 Baltimore Ave, Philadelphia, PA 19143.

"The Journey into Peacemaking" Glen Stassen. (1983) A thirteen session study, biblically based. Available from BAPTIST MEN, 1548 Poplar Avenue, Memphis TN 38104.

"How Beautiful Upon the Mountain" a three-session course on peacemaking and evangelism for congregations, and a six-session course on conflict management are available from the Presbyterian Distribution Center, Room 905, 475 Riverside Drive, New York, NY 10115. (201) 641-2528.

"SHALOM" is a 14-session study of the Biblical concept of peace available from The Kerygma Program, 300 Mt. Lebanon Blvd., Suite 205, Pittsburgh, PA 15234. (412) 344-6062.

"What about the Children?" ($1) and other materials are available from Parents and Teachers for Social Responsibility, Box 517, Moretown, VT 05660.

"Parenting for Peace and Justice" and "Partners in Peacemaking: Family Workshop Models" are available from the Parenting for Peace and Justice Network, Institute for Peace and Justice, 4144 Lindell, #400, St. Louis, MO 63108.

"Peace Education: A Bibliography focusing on Young Children" and other materials are available from Educators for Social Responsibility, 23 Garden Street, Cambridge, MA 02138.

Other materials particularly appropriate for use in schools and colleges may be found in the "Peace and World Order Studies: Curriculum Guide" available from the World Policy Institute, 777 United Nations Plaza, New York, NY 10017.

Peace Education Age-level Guidelines are available from Shalom Education, an Ecumenical Task Force on Christian Education for World Peace, 1448 East 53rd Street, Chicago, IL 60615. (312) 363-2020.

Audiovisuals:

(These are a few "starter" films, generally more hopeful in approach. They should be introduced and used in a setting where small groups can discuss them following the presentation.)

Gods of Metal analyzes the arms race from a Christian perspective, showing the economic effects and the actions of some groups attempting to stop the arms race. (27 minutes)

What about the Russians? uses expert testimony to explore the relative strength of the US and USSR. (26 minutes)

The Last Slide Show (filmstrip or slides) Effective treatment of the arms race ending on a hopeful note. (25 minutes)

These and other films may be available through your local library or Mass Media Ministries, 2116 N. Charles Street, Baltimore MD 21218. (301) 727-3270.

No Frames, No Boundaries a 21 minute video, is positive in approach and notes a number of grassroots actions towards building a world beyond war. Available for purchase with a discussion guide from Creative Initiatives, 222 High Street, Palo Alto, CA 94301. (415) 328-7756.

A videotape of the 1984 visit of 266 church people to the USSR called *On the Other Side* (52min, $17 rental) is available with a reader, "Together on the Way" from The John T. Conner Center for US-USSR reconciliation, 320 North Street, West Lafayette, IN 47906. Telephone 317-743-3861.

RESOURCE GUIDES

First Steps to Peace, (The Fund For Peace, Suite 207M, 345 East 46th Street, New York, NY 10017.) This 1985 guide is a very useful listing of a variety of peace education resources, from basic books to films to speakers. It has a special section on resources for use with children as well as one on specific resources for clergy and congregations. It is a handy introduction to materials beyond those listed here.

Many statements of denominations may be found in *To Proclaim Peace: Religious Communities Speak out on the Arms Race*, from the Fellowship of Reconciliation. Write: Fellowship Publications, Box 271, Nyack, NY 10960.

1984 National Directory of Audiovisual Resources on Nuclear War and the Arms Race," an extensive directory, is available from the University of Michigan, 400 Fourth Street, Ann Arbor, Michigan

PART III

Section B, Basic books dealing with male/female differences:

Bolen, Jean Shinoda. *Goddess in Everywoman* Harper and Row. 1984
Claremont de Castillejo, Irene. *Knowing Woman* Harper and Row. 1973
Dittes, James E., *The Male Predicament* Harper and Row. 1985
Gilligan, Carol. *In a Different Voice* Harvard University Press. 1982.
Levinson, Daniel. *The Seasons of a Man's Life* Alfred Knopf. 1978
May, Robert. *Sex and Fantasy.* W. W. Norton. 1980.
Miller, Jean Baker *Towards a New Psychology of Women* Beacon Press. 1976.

Noddings, Nel *Caring* University of California Press. 1984.
Reardon, Betty. *Sexism and the War System*. Columbia Teachers College. 1985.
Schaef, Anne Wilson *Woman's Reality* Winston Press. 1981.
Vaillant, George *Adaptation to Life* Little, Brown. 1977.
Washburn, Penelope *Becoming Woman* Harper and Row. 1977.

Section C (citation)

Reed, Bruce *The Task of The Church and The Role of Its Members* The Alban Institute. 1975.

APPENDIX:

(The following is reprinted from Action Information, Mar/April 1983)

A Safe Place to Face our Nuclear Terror, by R. T. Gribbon

What can congregations do in a practical way to help create a future in which there is less threat of nuclear war? Here are a few thoughts.

The new widespread public discussion of the nuclear threat comes as something of a surprise. We have lived in a nuclear age for some time now, and there have been people in the church who have been outspoken about peace and the nuclear realities, but the public awareness has apparently increased greatly in the past two years. People seem suddenly much more aware of the nuclear threat, and this awareness can have its own dangers. I believe that when people respond out of fear they reinforce their fear, do destructive things, or become paralyzed. One of the unique contributions that churches can make is hope. Hope for the future grounded in a believing, acting community can free people from the demonic effects of fear. As part of a faith community we act not simply to preserve the present order but in response to a vision of the "commonwealth of God" which may yet come "on earth as it is in heaven."

There are a number of organizations with resources on peacemaking in which one might participate, from "Ground Zero" to "The Christophers." Almost all the denominations have had peace witness groups within their midst for some time, and many of these are associated through one of the older interfaith peace witness groups in this country, the Fellowship of Reconciliation, Box 271, Nyack, New York 10960. Increasingly, regional and national church judicatories have created their own "peace commissions" or "peace resource groups." Many of these and the church-related publishing houses now provide good resources for peace-related education at the congregational level. Resources related to "parenting for peace and justice" seem particularly helpful because they tie the global concern for peace to the immediate concern that people have for their children. Our research in congregations indicates that most people do not deal with social issues except through the immediate and the concrete. For example, we see people become engaged in the issue of refugees through trying to find a home for one family. So too with the issue of peace; congregations need to find specific things people can do locally while thinking globally.

In our interviews with people of the baby-boom generation, I was surprised how few mentioned the possibility of war when asked directly, "When you think about the future (for yourself, people you care about, the world), what do you feel anxious or uneasy about?" But the threat of "the bomb" is something that my generation has lived with since our grade school days when we practiced the "duck and cover" drills in the hallways. When pressed, many have vivid memories of the Cuban missile crisis, while those of a somewhat older generation can recall feelings of uncomprehending awe when they first heard about this strange new weapon in 1945. Sharing these memories of fear that we have blocked from our everyday lives can be a first step towards living with courage in a dangerous time. If the parish is "a safe place to face our pain" (as Henri Nouwen put it in an earlier article in *Action Information*) it ought to be a place where we can face our repressed and taboo nuclear terror. At the same time, in sharing the stories we realize that we have a shared history which is a part of who we are as a community. I share with you from Chellis Glendinning's excellent article on "Telling Our Nuclear Stories" in *Fellowship*, the journal of the Fellowship of Reconciliation, her specific suggestions for creating a group in which people can tell their "nuclear stories" and thereby free energy to move creatively into the future.

Guidelines for Telling Your Story

What is needed to begin is permission, focus and support. If you want to initiate a group discussion, you might start with the group closest to you—your family, political organization, church, associates at work, or circle of friends. Then, if you wish, you can reach out to other groups or even offer a workshop to the public.

I have encouraged nuclear story-telling in many situations: in buses, at a large conference, in university classrooms, in cafes, at dinner parties, with individuals, with groups. The most important foundation for the experience is that the focus and methods be clearly drawn and agreed upon by all participants. This consensus provides the basis for safety. The focus is to share experience and feelings of living in the Nuclear Age. Methods may vary. If members of the group are accustomed to expressing deep feelings, they may want to cry or hit pillows as part of the telling. Or they may prefer to sit in straight back chairs and talk. They might like to make a special trip to the country for the sharing, or simply do it on their lunch hour at work.

Sitting in a circle is wise. As the tales come forth and we face their content and the feelings they elicit, we need the support that a circle seems to provide. It is easier to hold hands in a circle.

You may want to choose a facilitator and structure the group ... asking specific questions, one at a time, for group discussion. Or you may want to do what the eight peace activists in California did: have each person tell her/his own tale, one at a time.

The stories themselves are an intertwining of events, feelings and thoughts. Some important points to cover are:

History of Awareness: What are my earliest memories of nuclear weapons? What is the history of my awareness? When has it been greatest? When least? What important emotional experiences have I had that relate to nuclear weapons?

Psychic Numbing: How do I numb myself against the reality of nuclear weapons?

Coping: When I am not numbing myself, how do I cope with what I know?

Acknowledgement: If I have never explored my relationship to the nuclear situation, what have I learned by weaving this thread into my life story?

The Future: Where do I find support, strength and hope? Do I need more? Where can I find more?

Chellis Glendinning

(Reprinted with permission from Fellowship (12/81), a publication of the Fellowship for Reconciliation, Box 271, Nyack, New York 10960.)